KRISTIN HOULIHAN

Lift the Mask

a short collection of micropoetry and lyrical prose

For everyone who has encouraged me on my writing journey;
thank you for helping me believe I could do this.

Contents

Preface

Each of these short writings was originally posted on Twitter for a writing exercise called #vss365 (vss=very short story). The hashtagged word that makes up each chapter title indicates the one-word prompt for the day around which the poem or short piece of prose was written. I started out trying to write anything I could around the word—which is why earlier on you'll see some silly stories based on my grandparents—but eventually shifted to writing from the heart, only if and when the prompt struck me. The entries are presented in the order in which I wrote them, so you'll see my writing evolve as you read.

Acknowledgement

This short book wouldn't exist without the support and insights of so many people whom I'll try to call out here by name!

I need to say thank you to Kit Caelsto of Epona Author Solutions and Fiona West of Tempest and Kite Publishing for prompting this project; many thanks also to Fiona for the gorgeous cover and to my good friend Alison Solove for proofreading the finished book.

Thank you to the Twitter #vss365 community, to everyone who ever "liked" or commented on one of my posts and thus encouraged me to keep writing. Thank you also to the Twitter writing community writ large; I have learned so much from all of you, and rely so much on your practical and emotional support.

Thank you to my best friend, Gilda, whose conversation prompted the poem "Ubiquity," and who sent me a framed glass print of the poem: that gesture went further than any other toward making me feel like "a real writer."

To my children, who inspire so much of this and other writing, thank you for your boundless love and acceptance, for your support and excitement every time you see my name in a book.

Finally, much gratitude to my husband, Adam—nothing I do would exist without you. Thank you for living daily the words we vowed to one another sixteen years ago. You are my rock, my anchor in this storm of illness, parenting, faith, and life. Your physical and emotional support as I work through my experiences on the page are priceless. I love you.

#Grape

Just like every Easter, Grandma brought the roasted goat head to the table on a platter. I recoiled at the sight: head split down the middle, cooked brain on display. Grandpa smiled, using his fingers to pop the eye in his mouth. "Mmmmm, just like a #grape!"

#Peer; #Depression

I #peer up through the darkness, trying to judge how deep I've fallen. How long will it take to climb out this time? I take a deep breath and reach for the familiar handholds, dreading the journey up and out of the chasm. #Depression will lose. Again.

#Greenhorn

For just a moment, I revel in the feeling of being competent, maybe even good. In a heartbeat it's gone, fleeting, for children are ever-changing, ever-growing. I might find peace if I could embrace the inconvenient truth: I'll always be a #greenhorn.

#Rapier

"Chemical pregnancy." The two words, said with such indifference, acted as a #rapier through my soul, pierced by the denial of your very existence. But I know you were, you ARE. We had only a day before an agonizing goodbye, but I await the day our souls meet anew.

#Jazz

When we were new, I listened to you practice in the college music department. Still babies, we danced to Ella Fitzgerald singing Gershwin at our wedding. Fifteen years later you play #jazz piano in our living room, and I smile because I know Our Love Is Here To Stay.

#Ubiquity

Normalize the
   #ubiquity of brokenness.
   Enlighten all to the
   universality of struggle.
   Lift the mask worn
   by the apparently whole.
   Each broken soul
   will then find solace
   in knowing it's
   not alone.

#Obeisance

We bow,
    we kiss the Cross,
    we genuflect.
    Outward #obeisance,
    so often rote, habitual.
    Open our hearts,
    help us pour
    Your unconditional love out
    upon all humankind.
    For otherwise why are we here?
    Piety is nothing without
    radical love.

#Whose

The elderly couple sits in the backseat, hand-in-hand, as they've been for 55 years. The woman pulls a long, blonde hair off her husband's shirt. "#Whose is THIS?" she demands indignantly. With the hint of a smile and a twinkle in his eyes, he replies, "Some broad's."

#Bird

I watched her cradle the injured #bird in her hands, prepare for it a comfortable place to die—on this of all days. I cried as I marveled at her capacity to love, bonded to the chick by the nearness of death, the fragility of life. And I knew—she would survive.

#Halo

We crowned you an angel
　　because of your words,
　　your melodies.
　　For the creator of such beauty
　　must be eminently holy.
　　Alas, the music is
　　incongruent with the heart
　　from which it sprung.
　　The truth pierces the souls
　　of those who should know that
　　only God can give a #halo.

#Feel

I walked,
 bare feet slapping the pavement,
 thoughtless but for one repeating desire:
 to #feel.

I walked,
 floating through the fog
 and praying my bloodied feet
 would wake me from the
 emptiness.

#Watch

They somberly took the TV down from its mount, erased all traces of visual media in the house; if Mom's head exploded again the doctors might not be able to save her. Mom walked in, smiling. Then a kid yelled out, "Mom! We'll never ask 'Can we #watch something?' again!"

#Only

If #only
   anxiety would play
   by the rules of reason.

If only
   there were an answer
   to the oft-asked question—
   why are you anxious?

Then maybe
   I could predict
   or explain
   or understand
   why my body cries "danger"
   in the face of normalcy.

#Describe

I try to #describe
   the way I feel when
   anxiety dominates.
   Similes abound—I try some out
   but none can capture
   the horror
   of incessant noise.

#Storyteller

She'd spent years helping others hone their craft, perfect their words. Being a part of putting good writing into the world was fulfilling, and she was happy. Then one day it hit her: the urge to write. But was she—IS she—a #storyteller too?

#Everlasting

Powerful.
   All-encompassing.
   Unconditional.
   #Everlasting.

There is nothing
   my children can do
   that will change my love for them.

The loving comes easily,
   but knowing whether
   I've succeeded in
   conveying this truth
   feels impossible.

All I can do is try.

#Poleaxe

Grief is a #poleaxe
  to the heart
  that keeps coming
  but never kills,
  piercing anew,
  all-encompassing, unexpected agony
  always hovering,
  ready to strike its unsuspecting
  victim.

#Lazy

I remember
    the #lazy days
    of childhood,
    free to wander,
    to play,
    to explore—
    now I both envy
    and worry
    for my children,
    for their days
    are open-ended
    but their world
    is small.

#Crestfallen

#Crestfallen faces,
  worried hugs and kisses—
  the ever-present signs
  that my illness affects my children
  as much as me—
  hurt more than
  the bodily pain.
  My mother's heart
  longs for healing—
  for their sakes.

#Clear

She waits for the brain fog
   to #clear,
   for the familiar, comforting
   sharpness of thought
   to return,
   yearning to feel,
   however fleetingly,
   like the smart, capable
   woman she always
   used to be.

#Mock

I'd always offered
   compassion,
   at my best,
   indifference,
   at my worst:
   these, but never #mockery.

Until the disabled
   was me.

#Normalize

The realization of
  utopia
  is when there's
  nothing left to
  #normalize.

#Neighbors

It's hard to see others as #neighbors when you know nothing about them. You can hate the other more easily if they're strangers. Take the time to read, visit, learn, and it will be much easier to love.

#Shame

My #shame
    turns to indignation
    and then to anger
    as once again I hear,
    "Ma'am, everything checks
    out medically. Have you talked
    to psychology?
    You have a history..."

#Exist

Curtains drawn to shut out
　　the light,
　　I've become an observer, not
　　a participant.
　　My broken body struggles along,
　　a shadow
　　of its former self...
　　I #exist
　　but
　　I do not live.

#Unity

#Unity of soul and
  body,
  a composite being—
  what it means to be
  human.
  I must forgive this
  mutinous meat-suit
  if I am to
  love
  rather than
  hate
  myself.

#Dissonant

Where to go
    when the once-concordant
    songs of theology
    become #dissonant chords,
    clangingly proclaiming to be truth
    what now seems more like
    a hollow shell of platitudes?

#Pedestal

It's uncomfortable up here
   on this #pedestal.
   I worry for the day
   my children
   take me down,
   dust me off,
   and see my imperfections.
   If I'm halfway worthy
   of my place up here,
   they'll hug me close
   and love me just the same.

About the Author

I am a newly-disabled, chronically-ill editor-turned-writer. I write (mostly) poetry to make sense of and share my experiences from bedridden life with Myalgic Encephalomyclitis. I am blessed to share my life and home with my favorite five people: my husband and four children, who are an endless source of support and joy. I love books, the ocean, and listening to my family laugh together. (Photo Credit: Adam Houlihan)

You can connect with me on:
- https://kristinhoulihan.com
- https://twitter.com/theedifyingword

Subscribe to my newsletter:
- http://subscribepage.io/IsTb6g

Printed in Great Britain
by Amazon

40083262R10030